PIRATES!

HOP ON THE PIRATE HISTORY BOAT

Liam O'Donnell

raintree
a Capstone company — publishers for children

Raintree is an imprint of Capstone Global Library Limited, a company incorporated in England and Wales having its registered office at 264 Banbury Road, Oxford OX2 7DY – Registered company number: 6695582

www.raintree.co.uk
myorders@raintree.co.uk

Edited by Bradley Cole
Designed by Kayla Dohmen
Picture research by Wanda Winch
Production by Katy LaVigne
Originated by Capstone Global Library Ltd
Printed and bound in China

ISBN 978 1 4747 4542 0
22 21 20 19 18 17
10 9 8 7 6 5 4 3 2 1

British Library Cataloguing in Publication Data
A full catalogue record for this book is available from the British Library.

Acknowledgements
We would like to thank the following for permission to reproduce photographs: Alamy Stock Photo: Sami Sarkis, 25; Bridgeman Images: © Look and Learn/Private Collection/Graham Coton, 19, © Look and Learn/Private Collection/Roger Payne, 27, © Look and Learn/Private Collection/Ron Embleton, 15, Peter Newark Historical Pictures/Private Collection, 23, Peter Newark Historical Pictures/Private Collection/English School, 21, Private Collection/Howard Pyle, 17, The Stapleton Collection/Private Collection/Archibald Webb, 9; Getty Images Inc: Hulton Archive, 11; iStockphoto: AlexAndrews, cover (left), duncan1890, 7, JohnGollop, cover (background), Robert_Ford, 29; North Wind Picture Archives: Gerry Embleton, 13; Shutterstock: Andrey_Kuzmin, 2–3, parchment paper, Antony McAulay, 22, Evannovostro, cover (bottom right), Fer Gregory, cover (bottom left), ilolab, vintage paper texture, Marc Turcan, 5, Molodec, maps, Nik Merkulov, grunge background, pingebat, pirate icons, sharpner, map directions to island treasure, Triff, nautical background, TyBy, cover (banner)

Every effort has been made to contact copyright holders of material reproduced in this book. Any omissions will be rectified in subsequent printings if notice is given to the publisher.

All the Internet addresses (URLs) given in this book were valid at the time of going to press. However, due to the dynamic nature of the Internet, some addresses may have changed, or sites may have changed or ceased to exist since publication. While the author and publisher regret any inconvenience this may cause readers, no responsibility for any such changes can be accepted by either the author or the publisher.

CONTENTS

Some words are shown in bold, **like this**. You can find out what they mean by looking in the glossary.

Golden age of piracy

In the 1600s and early 1700s, thousands of men chose to become pirates. These men threatened ships and towns in the Caribbean and Mediterranean seas. This time became known as the Golden Age of Piracy.

Fact

The Caribbean islands were close to main shipping routes between Central America, South America and Europe.

Life as a navy sailor

Many pirates were once **navy** sailors. Life at sea was very difficult for them. They worked hard, lived in terrible conditions and got little pay. Navy captains could also be very cruel. They handed out harsh punishments to anyone who broke the rules.

Keelhauling was the worst punishment. A sailor was tied up and pulled under the ship. His body was cut by the sharp shells of **barnacles**. He often drowned.

Fact

Many sailors left the navy and became pirates just to escape keelhauling.

Sometimes, a **crew** would turn against their captain. This was called a mutiny. The captain was often killed or left alone on a **deserted** island. The crew took control of the ship and became pirates.

Fact

Oliver Ferneau was the captain of the **merchant ship** *George Galley*. In 1724, crewman John Gow threw Ferneau overboard. The ship became the pirate ship *Revenge*.

Why did sailors choose to be pirates?

Many men became pirates for one main reason – treasure! To a pirate, treasure was worth risking his life or even killing another person. Many pirates loved the excitement of attacking a ship and taking its treasure.

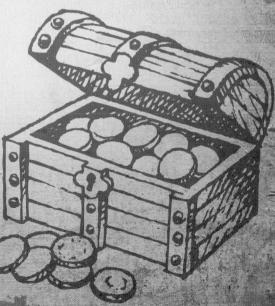

Fact

Pirates didn't win every battle. In 1722, "Black Bart" Roberts lost a battle against the *Swallow*, a British navy ship.

Although free from the navy, pirates still led rough lives. Their days were filled with hard work. They lived in uncomfortable conditions. Pirate ships were crowded, dirty and usually filled with disease. Boredom could also be a problem on long trips.

Fact

To pass the time, pirates often gambled on card games.

Government piracy

In the 1600s and 1700s, the only way to move anything over long distances was by ship. During wartime, many countries attacked enemy ships and stole their **cargo**. They used **privateers** to do this.

Fact

In the mid-1600s, Sir Henry Morgan worked as a privateer for the British government. He helped to capture Spanish ships in the Caribbean.

Governments gave **letters of marque** to **privateers**. A privateer was a man who owned his own ship. The letter said that he was allowed to attack ships that belonged to the country's enemies. In return, the privateer shared any treasure with the government.

Fact

In 1710, the Swedish king gave Lars Gathenhielm a letter of marque. Lars died in 1718. But his wife, Ingela, carried on the business.

By the early 1700s, many wars in Europe were over. **Privateers** were no longer allowed to rob ships. The peace was good for most people, but it was bad for privateers. They had no work and no money. Many privateers chose to become pirates.

Fact

In 1695, Captain William Kidd became a pirate hunter with his new ship, the *Adventure Galley*. But he couldn't find any pirates. So he decided to become one himself!

Different pirate types

Privateers sailed wherever they were needed to capture enemy ships. Ordinary pirates often threatened certain parts of the world. Corsairs roamed the Mediterranean Sea. Buccaneers usually attacked Spanish ships in the Caribbean Sea.

Fact

Henry Every was a pirate rounder. A rounder travelled around the Cape of Good Hope and attacked ships in the Indian Ocean.

Barbary corsairs were pirates who sailed the Mediterranean Sea in the early 1600s. Their favourite targets were Dutch ships. The corsairs first flew a Dutch flag from their **mast**. But when they got closer, they raised their pirate flag. The Dutch were often too shocked to fight back.

Fact

The corsairs captured 447 Dutch ships between 1613 and 1622.

23

In the 1600s, Spain controlled the island of Hispaniola. Many Frenchmen went there to hunt wild animals. These French buccaneers sometimes attacked ships sailing nearby.

To get rid of the buccaneers, Spain sent hunters to kill the animals. But instead of leaving, the hunters turned to piracy themselves.

Fact

The French hunters cooked meat on a wooden grill called a *boucan*. They became known as *boucaniers*, or "buccaneers".

Safe places

Around 1630, buccaneers settled on Tortuga Island off Hispaniola's coast. It had fresh water and safe **harbours**. However, France and Spain made peace in the 1690s. The pirates were driven away.

Buccaneers fled to Port Royal, Jamaica, instead. The English **governors** of the city welcomed the pirates because of the treasure they brought.

The end of piracy

By about 1750, most European countries were at peace. Pirates no longer roamed the seas raiding ships and attacking towns. The Golden Age of Piracy had come to an end.

Fact

Some treasure hunters think that gold and jewels still lie somewhere in the **harbour** at Port Royal. But no one has found treasure there – yet.

GLOSSARY

armed carrying weapons

barnacles small shellfish that are covered in very hard shells. They attach themselves to the sides of ships.

cargo goods carried by a ship from one country to another

crew group of people who work on a ship

deserted empty or abandoned

disease sickness or illness

gamble to bet money on the outcome of a race, game, or contest

governor person who runs a city or area

harbour place where ships load and unload passengers and cargo

letter of marque letter from a country's rulers that allowed privateers to attack and rob ships from enemy countries. They were allowed to keep part of any treasure they stole.

mast tall post on a ship to which sails are attached

merchant ship ship carrying items to sell

navy part of the armed services of a country that fights at sea, not on land

privateer sailor who is given permission by a government or other ruler to attack other ships

FIND OUT MORE

Books

Pirate Diary (Diary Histories), Richard Platt (Walker Books, 2014)

Pirate's Handbook, Sam Taplin (Usborne, 2014)

Pirates (Horrible Histories), Terry Deary (Scholastic, 2015)

Websites

www.dkfindout.com/uk/history/pirates
Want to know about pirates? This website will tell you all you need to know.

www.rmg.co.uk/discover/explore/life-and-times-pirate
Learn more about the lives of pirates on this website.

Places to visit

National Maritime Museum, Cornwall
Discovery Quay, Falmouth TR11 3QY
Learn all about the lives of people who have worked closely with the sea over the centuries at the National Maritime Museum.

INDEX